AF762103

Who are the Women in the Bible?

For my daughter,
who is everything these women are.
—Molly

For my mom and my daughter,
the kindest, most caring people I know.
—Shawnda

Text © 2025 Molly McNamara Carter
Art © 2025 Shawnda Craig
All rights reserved.

No part of this book may be reproduced in any form whatsoever, whether by graphic, visual, electronic, film, microfilm, tape recording, or any other means, without prior written permission of the publisher, except in the case of brief passages embodied in critical reviews and articles.

This is not an official publication of The Church of Jesus Christ of Latter-day Saints. The opinions and views expressed herein belong solely to the author and do not necessarily represent the opinions or views of Cedar Fort, Inc. Permission for the use of sources, graphics, and photos is also solely the responsibility of the author.

ISBN 13: 978-1-4621-4866-0

Published by CFI, an imprint of Cedar Fort, Inc.
2373 W. 700 S., Suite 100, Springville, UT 84663
Distributed by Cedar Fort, Inc., www.cedarfort.com

Library of Congress Control Number: 2025944319

Cover design and layout by Shawnda T. Craig
Cover design © 2025 Cedar Fort, Inc.
Edited by Kyle Lund

Printed in China

10 9 8 7 6 5 4 3 2

Printed on acid-free paper

Who are the Women in the Bible?

Written by Molly McNamara Carter • Art by Shawnda Craig

CFI • An imprint of Cedar Fort, Inc. • Springville, Utah

Who was the woman who
was first upon the earth?
She showed her strength
through sacrifice so we
could come by birth.

Eve!

Yes, Eve was the woman who
left a garden full of peace.
She knew that if she obeyed,
her joy would then increase.

Who was the woman whose great loyalty was shown? She left her land and traveled far, to a place unknown.

Ruth!

Yes, Ruth followed Naomi
to the Israelite Lands.
She chose to be obedient and
follow God's commands.

Who was the woman who
prayed to have a son
and promised he would serve
God until his days were done?

Hannah!

Yes, Hannah was blessed with the
child for whom she prayed.
She taught him to love God, and from
good he never strayed.

Who was the woman who was chosen to be queen? Her people would be killed if she did not intervene.

Esther!

Yes, Esther knew the danger
her choice would likely bring.
But with courage in her heart,
she stood before the king.

Who was the woman who
in the temple prayed?
God blessed her with a child
for the choices she made.

Elizabeth!

Yes, Elizabeth was the woman
who had faith and obeyed.
For Jesus's earthly mission, her
son John prepared the way.

Who was the mother
whose little baby lay,
wrapped in swaddling clothes
in a manger filled with hay?

Mary!

Yes, Mary was the mother of
Jesus Christ our Lord.
She taught Him and protected
Him, the child she adored.

Who were the sisters who
listened to Jesus preach?
They helped and
cared for him, so that
he could teach.

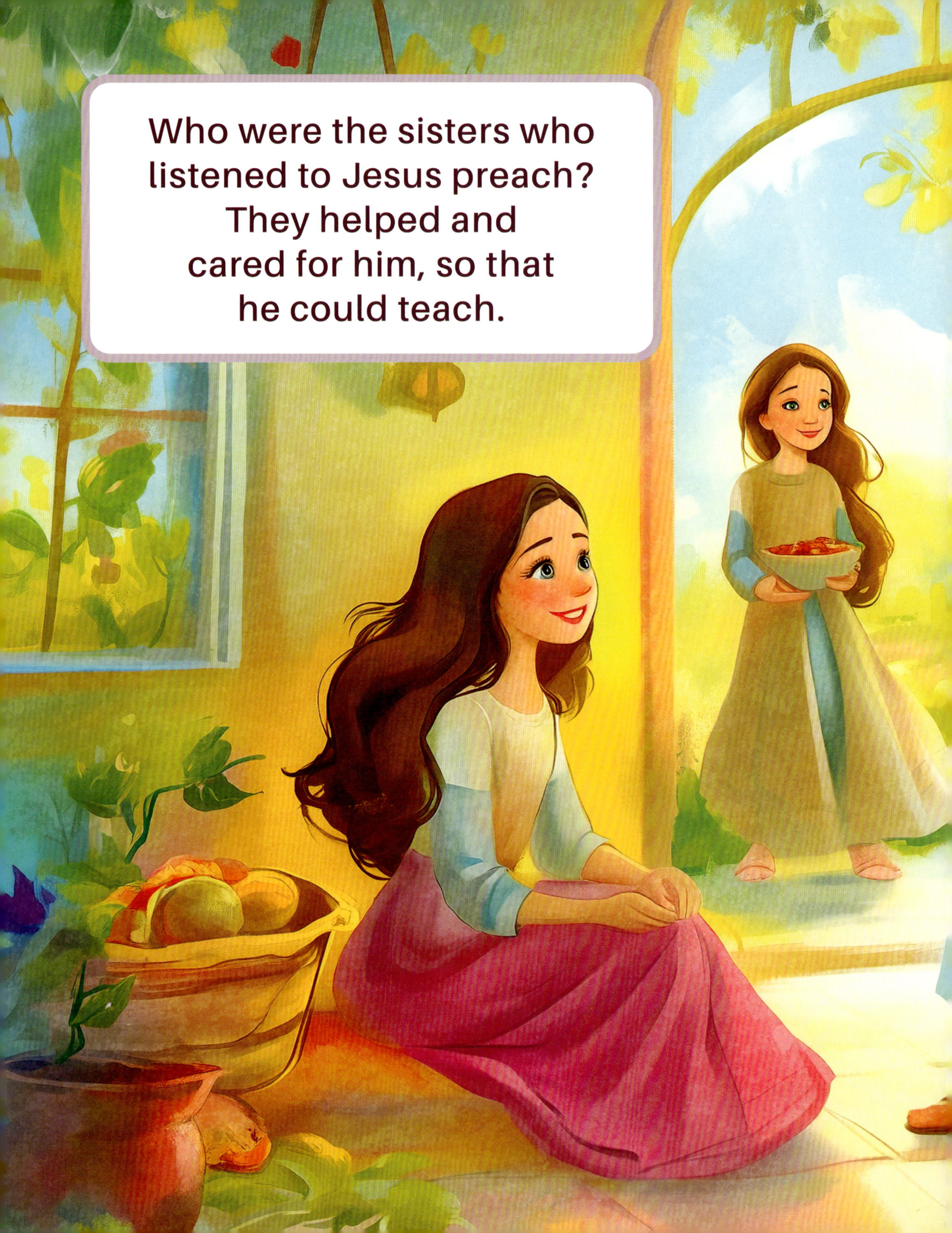

Mary and Martha!

Yes, Mary and Martha were the sisters
whose faith filled them with awe.
They were his friends and loved him,
and miracles they saw.

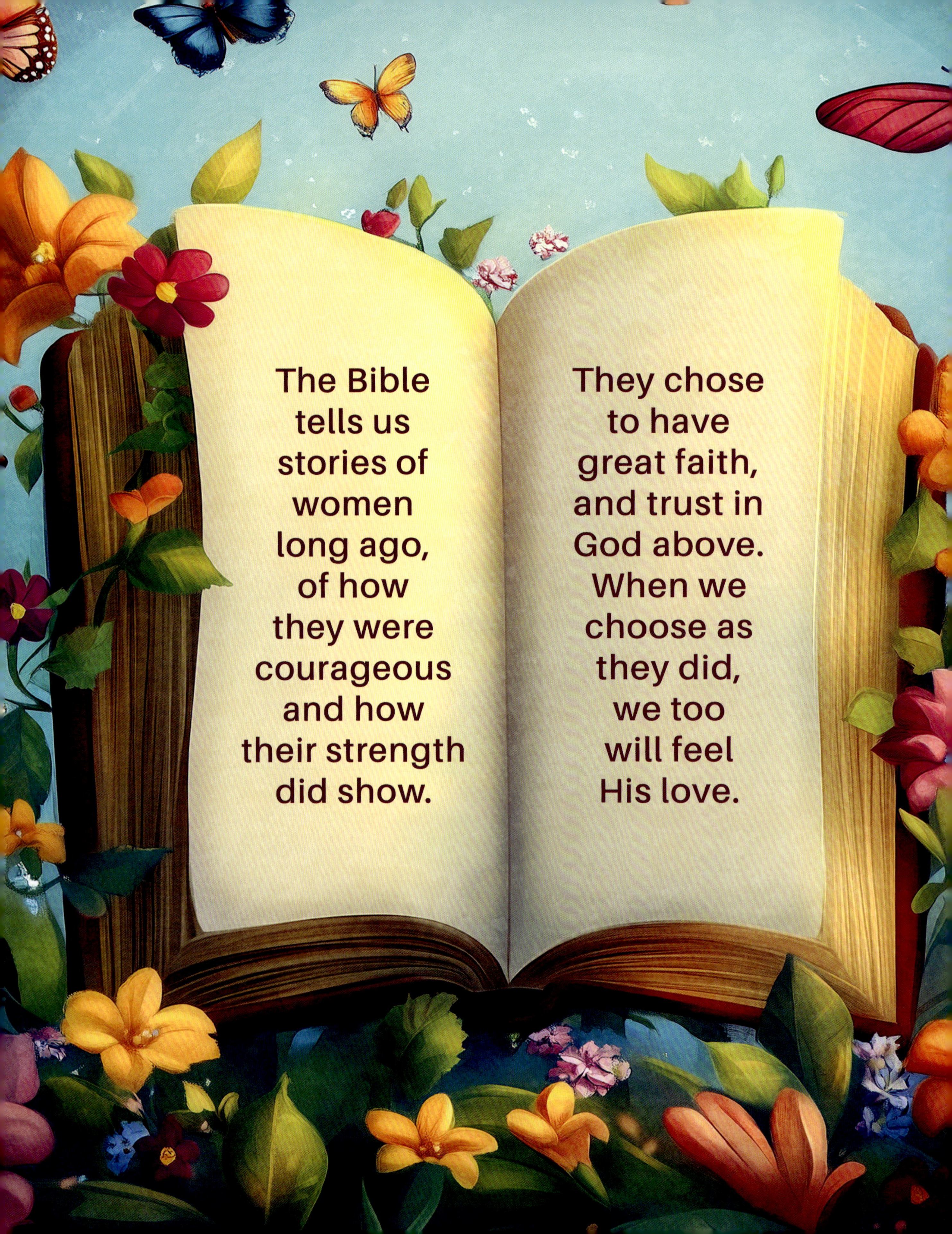

The Bible
tells us
stories of
women
long ago,
of how
they were
courageous
and how
their strength
did show.

They chose
to have
great faith,
and trust in
God above.
When we
choose as
they did,
we too
will feel
His love.